THE

ROMANTIC SCOTTISH BALLADS:

THEIR

EPOCH AND AUTHORSHIP.

ROBERT CHAMBERS.

1849

THE

ROMANTIC SCOTTISH BALLADS:

THEIR
EPOCH AND AUTHORSHIP.

ROBERT CHAMBERS.

THE ROMANTIC SCOTTISH BALLADS: THEIR EPOCH AND AUTHORSHIP.

Percy's *Reliques of Ancient English Poetry,* 1765; David Herd's *Scottish Songs,* 1769; Scott's *Minstrelsy of the Scottish Border,* 1802; and Jamieson's *Popular Ballads and Songs,* 1806, have been chiefly the means of making us acquainted with what is believed to be the ancient traditionary ballad literature of Scotland; and this literature, from its intrinsic merits, has attained a very great fame. I advert particularly to what are usually called the Romantic Ballads, a class of compositions felt to contain striking beauties, almost peculiar to themselves, and consequently held as implying extraordinary poetical attributes in former generations of the people of this country. There have been many speculations about the history of these poems, all assigning them a considerable antiquity, and generally assuming that their recital was once the special business of a set of wandering *conteurs* or minstrels. So lately as 1858, my admired friend, Professor Aytoun, in introducing a collection of them, at once ample and elegant, to the world, expressed his belief that they date at least from before the Reformation, having only been modified by successive reciters, so as to modernise the language, and, in some instances, bring in the ideas of later ages.

There is, however, a sad want of clear evidence regarding the history of our romantic ballads. We have absolutely no certain knowledge of them before 1724, when Allan Ramsay printed one called *Sweet William's Ghost,* in his *Tea-table Miscellany.* There is also this fact staring us in the face, that, while these poems refer to an ancient state of society, they bear not the slightest resemblance either to the minstrel poems of the middle ages, or to the well-known productions of the Henrysons, the Dunbars, the Douglases, the Montgomeries, who flourished in the fifteenth and sixteenth centuries. Neither in the poems of Drummond, and such other specimens of verse—generally wretched—as existed in the seventeenth century, can we trace any feature of the composition of these ballads. Can it be that all editors hitherto have been too facile in accepting them as ancient, though modified compositions? that they are to a much greater extent modern than has hitherto been supposed? or wholly so? Though in early life an editor of them, not less trusting than any of my predecessors, I must own that a suspicion regarding their age and authorship has at length entered my mind. In stating it—which I do in a spirit of great deference to Professor Aytoun and others—I shall lead the reader through the steps by which I arrived at my present views upon the subject.

In 1719, there appeared, in a folio sheet, at Edinburgh, a heroic poem styled *Hardyknute,* written in affectedly old spelling, as if it had been a contemporary description of events connected with the invasion of Scotland by Haco, king of Norway, in 1263. A corrected copy was soon after presented in the *Evergreen* of Allan Ramsay, a collection professedly of poems written before 1600, but into which we know the editor admitted a piece written by himself. *Hardyknute* was afterwards reprinted in Percy's *Reliques,* still as an ancient composition; yet it was soon after declared to be the production of a Lady Wardlaw of Pitreavie, who died so lately as 1727. Although, to modern taste, a stiff and poor composition, there is a nationality of feeling about it, and a touch of chivalric spirit, that has maintained for it a certain degree of popularity. Sir Walter Scott tells us it was the first poem he ever learned by heart, and he believed it would be the last he should forget.

It is necessary to present a few brief extracts from this poem. In the opening, the Scottish king, Alexander III., is represented as receiving notice of the Norwegian invasion:

The king of Norse, in summer pride,
Puffed up with power and micht,
Landed in fair Scotland, the isle,
With mony a hardy knicht.
The tidings to our gude Scots king
Came as he sat at dine,

With noble chiefs in brave array,
Drinking the blude-red wine.
'To horse, to horse, my royal liege;
Your faes stand on the strand;
Full twenty thousand glittering spears
The king of Norse commands.'
'Bring me my steed, page, dapple-gray,'
Our good king rose and cried;
'A trustier beast in a' the land
A Scots king never tried.'

Hardyknute, summoned to the king's assistance, leaves his wife and daughter, 'Fairly fair,' under the care of his youngest son. As to the former lady—

... first she wet her comely cheeks,
And then her bodice green,
Her silken cords of twirtle twist,
Well plet with silver sheen;
And apron, set with mony a dice
Of needle-wark sae rare,
Wove by nae hand, as ye may guess,
But that of Fairly fair.

In his journey, Hardyknute falls in with a wounded and deserted knight, to whom he makes an offer of assistance:

With smileless look and visage wan,
The wounded knight replied:
'Kind chieftain, your intent pursue,
For here I maun abide.
'To me nae after day nor nicht
Can e'er be sweet or fair;
But soon beneath some dropping tree,
Cauld death shall end my care.'

A field of battle is thus described:

In thraws of death, with wallowit cheek,
All panting on the plain,
The fainting corps[1] of warriors lay,

[1] A Scotticism, plural of corp, a body.

Ne'er to arise again;
Ne'er to return to native land,
Nae mair, with blithesome sounds,
To boast the glories of the day,
And shaw their shining wounds.
On Norway's coast, the widowed dame
May wash the rock with tears,
May lang look o'er the shipless seas,
Before her mate appears.
'Cease, Emma, cease to hope in vain;
Thy lord lies in the clay;
The valiant Scots nae rievers thole [2]
To carry life away.'

I must now summon up, for a comparison with these specimens of the modern antique in ballad lore, the famous and admired poem of *Sir Patrick Spence*. It has come to us mainly through two copies—one comparatively short, published in Percy's *Reliques*, as 'from two manuscript copies transmitted from Scotland;' the other, containing more details, in Scott's *Minstrelsy of the Scottish Border*, also 'from two manuscript copies,' but 'collated with several verses recited by the editor's friend, Robert Hamilton, Esq., advocate.' It is nowhere pretended that any *ancient* manuscript of this poem has ever been seen or heard of. It acknowledgedly has come to us from modern manuscripts, as it might be taken down from modern reciters; although Percy prints it in the same quasi antique spelling as that in which *Hardyknute* had appeared, where being *quhar*; sea, *se*; come, *cum*; year, *zeir*; &c. It will be necessary here to reprint the whole ballad, as given originally by Percy, introducing, however, within brackets the additional details of Scott's copy: [3]

The king sits in Dunfermline town,
Drinking the blude-red wine:
'O whar will I get a gude sailòr,

---

[2] Permit no robbers, &c.

[3] Only omitting the five verses supplied by Mr Hamilton, as they appear redundant.

To sail this ship of mine?'
Up and spak an eldern knight,
Sat at the king's right knee:
'Sir Patrick Spence is the best sailòr
That sails upon the sea.'
The king has written a braid letter,
And signed it with his hand,
And sent it to Sir Patrick Spence,
Was walking on the sand.
['To Noroway, to Noroway,
To Noroway o'er the faem;
The king's daughter of Noroway,
'Tis thou maun bring her hame.']
The first line that Sir Patrick read,
A loud lauch lauched he:
The next line that Sir Patrick read,
The tear blinded his ee.
'O wha is this hae done this deed,
This ill deed done to me;
To send me out this time o' the year,
To sail upon the sea?
['Be it wind, be it weet, be it hail, be it sleet,
Our ship must sail the faem;
The king's daughter of Noroway,
'Tis we must fetch her hame.'
They hoysed their sails on Monenday morn,
Wi' a' the speed they may;
They hae landed in Noroway,
Upon a Wodensday.
They had na been a week, a week,
In Noroway, but twae,
When that the lords of Noroway
Began aloud to say:
'Ye Scottish men spend a' our king's gowd,
And a' our queenis fee.'
'Ye lie, ye lie, ye liars loud,

Fu' loud I hear ye lie.
'For I hae broucht as much white monie
As gane[4] my men and me,
And I broucht a half-fou o' gude red gowd,
Out ower the sea wi' me.']
'Mak haste, mak haste, my merry men a',
Our gude ship sails the morn.'
'O say na sae, my master dear,[5]
For I fear a deadly storm.
'Late, late yestreen, I saw the new moon
Wi' the auld moon in her arm;
And I fear, I fear, my master dear,
That we will come to harm.'
[They had na sailed a league, a league,
A league but barely three,
When the lift grew dark, and the wind blew loud,
And gurly grew the sea.
The ankers brak, and the topmasts lap,
It was sic a deadly storm,
And the waves cam o'er the broken ship,
Till a' her sides were torn.]
O our Scots nobles were richt laith
To weet their cork-heeled shoon;
But lang ere a' the play was played,
Their hats they swam aboon. [6]
[And mony was the feather-bed
That flattered on the faem;
And mony was the gude lord's son
That never mair cam hame.
The ladies wrang their fingers white,
The maidens tore their hair,

---

[4] Serve.

[5] Variation in Scott:
Now ever alake, my master dear.

[6] Variation in Scott:
They wet their hats aboon.

A' for the sake of their true loves,
For them they'll see nae mair.]
O lang, lang may the ladies sit,
Wi' their fans into their hand,
Or ere they see Sir Patrick Spence
Come sailing to the land.
O lang, lang may the ladies stand,
Wi' their gold kames in their hair,
Waiting for their ain dear lords,
For they'll see them nae mair.
Half ower, half ower to Aberdour,[7]
It's fifty fathom deep;
And there lies gude Sir Patrick Spence
Wi' the Scots lords at his feet.

Percy, at the close of his copy of *Sir Patrick Spence*, tells us that 'an ingenious friend' of his was of opinion that 'the author of *Hardyknute* has borrowed several expressions and sentiments from the foregoing [ballad], and other old Scottish songs in this collection.' It does not seem to have ever occurred to the learned editor, or any friend of his, however 'ingenious,' that perhaps *Sir Patrick Spence* had no superior antiquity over *Hardyknute*, and that the parity he remarked in the expressions was simply owing to the two ballads being the production of one mind. Neither did any such suspicion occur to Scott. He fully accepted *Sir Patrick Spence* as a historical narration, judging it to refer most probably to an otherwise unrecorded embassy to bring home the Maid of Norway, daughter of King Eric, on the succession to the Scottish crown opening to her in 1286, by the death of her grandfather, King Alexander III., although the names of the ambassadors who did go for that purpose are known to have been different.[8] The

[7] Variation in Scott:
O forty miles off Aberdeen.

[8] There is one insuperable objection to Sir Walter's theory, which I am surprised should not have occurred to himself, or to some of those who have followed him. In his version of the ballad, the design to bring home the daughter of the king of Norway is expressed by the king of Scotland himself.

want of any ancient manuscript, the absence of the least trait of an ancient style of composition, the palpable modernness of the diction—for example, 'Our ship must sail the faem,' a glaring specimen of the poetical language of the reign of Queen Anne—and, still more palpably, of several of the things alluded to, as cork-heeled shoon, hats, fans, and feather-beds, together with the inapplicableness of the story to any known event of actual history, never struck any editor of Scottish poetry, till, at a recent date, Mr David Laing intimated his suspicions that *Sir Patrick Spence* and *Hardyknute* were the production of the same author.[9] To me it appears that there could not well be more remarkable traits of an identity of authorship than what are presented in the extracts given from *Hardyknute* and the entire poem of *Sir Patrick*—granting only that the one poem is a considerable improvement upon the other. Each poem opens with absolutely the same set of particulars—a Scottish king sitting—drinking the blude-red

---

Now, there was no occasion for Alexander III. sending for his infant granddaughter; nor is it conceivable that, in his lifetime, such a notion should have occurred or been entertained on either his side or that of the child's father. It was not till after the death of Alexander had made the infant Norwegian princess queen of Scotland—four years after that event, indeed—that the *guardians of the kingdom*, in concert with Edward I. of England, sent for her by Sir David Wemyss of Wemyss and Sir Michael Scott of Balwearie, who actually brought her home, but in a dying state. For these reasons, on the theory of the ballad referring to a real occurrence, it must have been to the bringing home of some Norwegian princess to be wedded to a king of Scotland that it referred. *But there is no such event in Scottish history.*
Professor Aytoun alters a verse of the ballad as follows:

To Noroway, to Noroway,
To Noroway o'er the faem;
The king's daughter *to* Noroway,
It's thou maun tak her hame.

And he omits the verse in which Sir Patrick says:

The king's daughter of Noroway,
'Tis we must fetch her hame.

Thus making the ballad referrible to the expedition in 1281 for taking Alexander's daughter to be married to the king of Norway. But I apprehend such liberties with an old ballad are wholly unwarrantable.

[9] Notes to Johnson's *Scots Musical Museum*, 1839.

wine—and sending off a message to a subject on a business of importance. Norway is brought into connection with Scotland in both cases. Sir Patrick's exclamation, 'To Noroway, to Noroway,' meets with an exact counterpart in the 'To horse, to horse,' of the courtier in *Hardyknute*. The words of the ill-boding sailor in *Sir Patrick*, 'Late, late yestreen, I saw the new moon'—a very peculiar expression, be it remarked—are repeated in *Hardyknute*:

'Late, late the yestreen I weened in peace,'
To end my lengthened life.'

The grief of the ladies at the catastrophe in *Sir Patrick Spence*, is equally the counterpart of that of the typical Norse lady with regard to the fate of her male friend at Largs. I am inclined, likewise, to lay some stress on the localities mentioned in *Sir Patrick Spence*—namely, Dunfermline and Aberdour—these being places in the immediate neighbourhood of the mansions where Lady Wardlaw spent her maiden and her matron days. A poet, indeed, often writes about places which he never saw; but it is natural for him to be most disposed to write about those with which he is familiar; and some are first inspired by the historical associations connected with their native scenes. True, as has been remarked, there is a great improvement upon *Hardyknute* in the 'grand old ballad of *Sir Patrick Spence*,' as Coleridge calls it, yet not more than what is often seen in compositions of a particular author at different periods of life. It seems as if the hand which was stiff and somewhat puerile in *Hardyknute*, had acquired freedom and breadth of style in *Sir Patrick Spence*. For all of these reasons, I feel assured that *Sir Patrick* is a modern ballad, and suspect, or more than suspect, that the author is Lady Wardlaw. [10]

---

[10] Professor Aytoun says: 'It is true that the name [of Sir Patrick Spence] ... is not mentioned in history: but I am able to state that tradition has preserved it. In the little island of Papa Stronsay, one of the Orcadian group, lying over against Norway, there is a large grave or tumulus, which has been known to the inhabitants from time immemorial as "The grave of Sir Patrick Spence." The Scottish ballads were not early current in Orkney, a Scandinavian country; to it is very unlikely that the poem could have originated the name.' I demur to this unlikelihood, and would require some proof to convince me that the grave of

Probably, by this time, the reader will desire to know what is now to be known regarding Lady Wardlaw. Unfortunately, this is little, for, as she shrank from the honours of authorship in her lifetime, no one thought of chronicling anything about her. We learn that she was born Elizabeth Halket, being the second daughter of Sir Charles Halket of Pitfirran, Baronet, who was raised to that honour by Charles II., and took an active part, as a member of the Convention of 1689, in settling the crown upon William and Mary. Her eldest sister, Janet, marrying Sir Peter Wedderburn of Gosford, was the progenitress of the subsequent Halkets, baronets of Pitfirran, her son being Sir Peter Halket, colonel of the 44th regiment of foot, who died in General Braddock's unfortunate conflict at Monongahela in 1755. A younger sister married Sir John Hope Bruce of Kinross, baronet, who died, one of the oldest lieutenant-generals in the British service, in 1766. Elizabeth, the authoress of *Hardyknute*, born on the 15th of April 1677, became, in June 1696, the wife of Sir Henry Wardlaw of Pitreavie (third baronet of the title), to whom she bore a son, subsequently fourth baronet, and three daughters. [11]

The ballad of *Hardyknute*, though printed in a separate brochure by James Watson in 1719, had been previously talked of or quoted, for the curiosity of Lord Binning was excited about it, apparently in a conversation with Sir John Hope Bruce, the brother-in-law of Lady Wardlaw. Pinkerton received from Lord Hailes, and printed, an extract from a letter of Sir John to Lord Binning, as follows: 'To perform my promise, I send you a true copy of the manuscript I found a few weeks ago in a vault at Dunfermline. It is written on vellum, in a fair Gothic character, but so much defaced by time as you'll find the tenth part not legible.' Sir John, we are told by Pinkerton, transcribed in this letter 'the whole fragment first published, save one or two stanzas,

---

Sir Patrick Spence in Papa Stronsay is not a parallel geographical phenomenon to the island of Ellen Douglas in Loch Katrine.

[11] Playfair's *Brit. Fam. Antiquity*, viii., 170, lxviii.

marking several passages as having perished, from being illegible in the old manuscript.' [12]

Here is documentary evidence that *Hardyknute* came out through the hands of Lady Wardlaw's brother-in-law, with a story about its discovery as an old manuscript, so transparently fictitious, that one wonders at people of sense having ever attempted to obtain credence for it—which consequently forms in itself a presumption as to an authorship being concealed. Pinkerton rashly assumed that Sir John Bruce was the author of the poem, and on the strength of that assumption, introduced his name among the Scottish poets.

The first hint at the real author came out through Percy, who, in his second edition of the *Reliques* (1767), gives the following statement:

'There is more than reason to suspect that it [*Hardyknute*] owes most of its beauties (if not its whole existence) to the pen of a lady within the present century. The following particulars may be depended on. Mrs [mistake for Lady] Wardlaw, whose maiden name was Halket ... pretended she had found this poem, written on shreds of paper, employed for what is called the bottoms of clues. A suspicion arose that it was her own composition. Some able judges asserted it to be modern. The lady did in a manner acknowledge it to be so. Being desired to show an additional stanza, as a proof of this, she produced the two last, beginning with "There's nae light, &c.," which were not in the copy that was first printed. The late Lord President Forbes and Sir Gilbert Elliot of Minto (late Lord Justice-clerk for Scotland), who had believed it ancient, contributed to the expense of publishing the first edition, in folio, 1719. This account was transmitted from Scotland by Sir David Dalrymple (Lord Hailes),[13] who yet was of opinion that part of the ballad may be ancient, but retouched and

---

[12] *Ancient Scottish Poems*, 2 vols. (1786), i. p. cxxvii.

[13] It is rather remarkable that Percy was not informed of these particulars in 1765; but in 1767—*Sir John Hope Bruce having died in the interval* (June 1766)—they were communicated to him. It looks as if the secret had hung on the life of this venerable gentleman.

much enlarged by the lady above mentioned. Indeed, he had been informed that the late William Thomson, the Scottish musician, who published the *Orpheus Caledonius*, 1733, declared he had heard fragments of it repeated in his infancy before Mrs Wardlaw's copy was heard of.'

The question as to the authorship of *Hardyknute* was once more raised in 1794, when Sir Charles Halket, grandson of Mary, third daughter of Lady Wardlaw, wrote a letter to Dr Stenhouse of Dunfermline, containing the following passage: 'The late Mr Hepburn of Keith often declared he was in the house with Lady Wardlaw when she wrote *Hardyknute*.' He also gave the following particulars in a manuscript account of his family, as reported by George Chalmers (*Life of Allan Ramsay*, 1800): 'Miss Elizabeth Menzies, daughter of James Menzies, Esq., of Woodend, in Perthshire, by Elizabeth, the daughter of Sir Henry Wardlaw [second baronet], wrote to Sir Charles Halket that her mother, who was sister-in-law to Lady Wardlaw, told her that Lady Wardlaw was the real authoress of *Hardyknute*; that Mary, the wife of Charles Wedderburn, Esq., of Gosford, told Miss Menzies that her mother, Lady Wardlaw, wrote *Hardyknute*. Sir Charles Halket and Miss Elizabeth Menzies concur in saying that Lady Wardlaw was a woman of elegant accomplishments, *who wrote other poems*, and practised drawing, and cutting paper with her scissors, and *who had much wit and humour*, with great sweetness of temper.'

In the middle of the last century appeared two editions of a brochure containing the now well-known ballad of *Gil Morrice*; the date of the second was 1755. Prefixed to both was an advertisement setting forth that the preservation of this poem was owing 'to a lady, who favoured the printers with a copy, as it was carefully collected from the mouths of old women and nurses;' and 'any reader that can render it more correct or complete,' was desired to oblige the public with such improvements. Percy adopted the poem into his collection, with four additional verses, which meanwhile had been 'produced and handed about in manuscript,' but which were in a florid style, glaringly incongruous with the rest of the piece. He at the same time mentioned that there existed, in his folio manuscript, (supposed) of Elizabeth's time, an imperfect copy of the same ballad, under the title of *Child Maurice.*

This early ballad of *Child Maurice,* which Mr Jamieson afterwards printed from Percy's manuscript, gives the same story of a gentleman killing, under jealousy, a young man, who proved to be a son of his wife by a former connection. But it is a poor, bald, imperfect composition, in comparison with *Gil Morrice.* It was evident to Percy that there had been a '*revisal*' of the earlier poem, attended by '*considerable improvements.*'

Now, by whom had this improving revisal been effected? Who was the 'lady' that favoured the printers with the copy? I strongly suspect that the reviser was Lady Wardlaw, and that the poem was communicated to the printers either by her or by some of her near relations. The style of many of the verses, and even some of the particular expressions, remind us strongly of *Sir Patrick Spence*; while other verses, again, are more in the stiff manner of *Hardyknute.* The poem opens thus:

Gil Morrice was an earl's son,
His name it waxed wide;
It was na for his great riches,
Nor yet his mickle pride;
But it was for a lady gay,
That lived on Carron side.
'Whar sall I get a bonny boy,
That will win hose and shoon;
That will gae to Lord Barnard's ha',
And bid his lady come?
'And ye maun rin my errand, Willie,
And ye may rin wi' pride,
When other boys gae on their foot,
On horseback ye sall ride.'
'O no! O no! my master dear,
I dare nae for my life;
I'll ne gae to the bauld baron's,

For to tryst forth his wife.'
'O say na sae, my master dear,
For I fear a deadly storm.'

What next follows is like *Hardyknute*:

'But, O my master dear,' he cried,
In green wood ye're your lane;
Gie ower sic thoughts, I wad ye reid,
For fear ye should be tane.'
'Haste, haste! I say, gae to the ha';
Bid her come here wi' speed:
If ye refuse my heigh command,
I'll gar your body bleed.'

When the boy goes in and pronounces the fatal message before Lord Barnard:

Then up and spak the wily nurse,
The bairn upon her knee:
'If it be come frae Gil Morrice,
It's dear welcome to me.'

Compare this with the second verse of *Sir Patrick Spence*:

O up and spak an eldern knight,
Sat at the king's right knee, &c.

The messenger replies to the nurse:

'Ye lied, ye lied, ye filthy nurse,
Sae loud I heard ye lie,' &c.

Identical with Sir Patrick's answer to the taunt of the Norwegian lords:

'Ye lie, ye lie, ye liars loud,
Fu' loud I hear ye lie.'

When the youth has been slain by Lord Barnard, the lady explains that he was her son, and exclaims:

'To me nae after days nor nichts
Will e'er be saft or kind;
I'll fill the air wi' heavy sighs,
And greet till I am blind.'

How nearly is this the same with the doleful complaint of the wounded knight in *Hardyknute*!

'To me nae after day nor night
Can e'er be sweet or fair,' &c.

Lord Barnard pours out his contrition to his wife:

'With waefu' wae I hear your plaint,
Sair, sair I rue the deed,
That e'er this cursed hand of mine
Had garred his body bleed.'

'Garred his body bleed' is a quaint and singular expression: it occurs in *Hardyknute*, and nowhere else:

'To lay thee low as horse's hoof,
My word I mean to keep:'
Syne with the first stroke e'er he strake,
He garred his body bleed.

Passages and phrases of one poem appear in another from various causes—plagiarism and imitation; and in traditionary lore, it is easy to understand how a number of phrases might be in general use, as part of a common stock. But the parallel passages above noted are confined to a particular group of ballads—they are not to such an extent *beauties* as to have been produced by either plagiarism or imitation; it is submitted that they thus appear by an overwhelmingly superior likelihood as the result of a common authorship in the various pieces.

Having so traced a probable common authorship, and that modern, from *Hardyknute* to *Sir Patrick Spence*, and from these two to the revised and improved edition of *Gil Morrice*, I was tempted to inquire if there be not others of the Scottish ballads liable to similar suspicion as to the antiquity of their origin? May not the conjectured author of these three have written several of the remainder of that group of compositions, so remarkable as they likewise are for their high literary qualities? Now, there is in Percy a number of Scottish ballads equally noteworthy for their beauty, and for the way in which they came to the hands of the editor. There is *Edward, Edward*, 'from a manuscript copy transmitted from Scotland;' the *Jew's Daughter*, 'from a manuscript copy sent from Scotland;' *Gilderoy*, 'from a written copy that appears to have received some modern corrections;'

likewise, *Young Waters*, 'from a copy printed not long since at Glasgow, in one sheet octavo,' for the publication of which the world was 'indebted to Lady Jean Home, sister to the Earl of Home;' and *Edom o' Gordon*, which had been put by Sir David Dalrymple to Foulis's press in 1755, 'as it was preserved in the memory of a lady that is now dead'—Percy, however, having in this case improved the ballad by the addition of a few stanzas from a fragment in his folio manuscript. Regarding the *Bonny Earl of Murray*, the editor tells us nothing beyond calling it 'a Scottish song.' Of not one of these seven ballads, as published by Percy, has it ever been pretended that any ancient manuscript exists, or that there is any proof of their having had a being before the eighteenth century, beyond the rude and dissimilar prototypes (shall we call them?) which, *in two instances*, are found in the folio manuscript of Percy. No person was cited at first as having been accustomed to recite or sing them; and they have not been found familiar to the common people since. Their style is elegant, and free from coarsenesses, while yet exhibiting a large measure of the ballad simplicity. In all literary grace, they are as superior to the generality of the homely traditionary ballads of the rustic population, as the romances of Scott are superior to a set of chap-books. Indeed, it might not be very unreasonable to say that these ballads have done more to create a popularity for Percy's *Reliques* than all the other contents of the book. There is a community of character throughout all these poems, both as to forms of expression and style of thought and feeling—jealousy in husbands of high rank, maternal tenderness, tragic despair, are prominent in them, though not in them all. In several, there is the same kind of obscure and confused reference to known events in Scottish history, which editors have thought they saw in *Sir Patrick Spence*.

Let us take a cursory glance at these poems.

Young Waters is a tale of royal jealousy. It is here given entire.

About Yule, when the wind blew cool,
And the round tables began,

A! there is come to our king's court
Mony a well-favoured man.
The queen looked ower the castle-wa',
Beheld baith dale and down,
And then she saw Young Waters
Come riding to the town.
His footmen they did rin before,
His horsemen rade behind,
Ane mantel o' the burning gowd
Did keep him frae the wind.
Gowden graithed his horse before,
And siller shod behind;
The horse Young Waters rade upon
Was fleeter than the wind.
But then spak a wily lord,
Unto the queen said he:
'O tell me wha's the fairest face
Rides in the company?'
'I've seen lord, and I've seen laird,
And knights of high degree;
But a fairer face than Young Waters
Mine een did never see.'
Out then spak the jealous king,
And an angry man was he:
'O if he had been twice as fair,
You might have excepted me.'
'You're neither lord nor laird,' she says,
'But the king that wears the crown;
There's not a knight in fair Scotland,
But to thee maun bow down.'
For a' that she could do or say,
Appeased he wadna be,
But for the words which she had said,
Young Waters he maun dee.
They hae tane Young Waters, and
Put fetters to his feet;

They hae tane Young Waters, and
Thrown him in dungeon deep.
Aft hae I ridden through Stirling town,
In the wind but and the weet,
But I ne'er rade through Stirling town
Wi' fetters at my feet.
Aft hae I ridden through Stirling town,
In the wind both and the rain,
But I ne'er rade through Stirling town
Ne'er to return again.
They hae tane to the heading-hill
His young son in his cradle;
They hae tane to the heading-hill
His horse both and his saddle.
They hae tane to the heading-hill
His lady fair to see;
And for the words the queen had spoke,
Young Waters he did dee.

Now, let the parallel passages be here observed. In verse second, the lady does exactly like the mother of Gil Morrice, of whom it is said:

The lady sat on the castle-wa',
Beheld baith dale and down,
And there she saw Gil Morrice' head
Come trailing to the town.

Dale and down, let it be observed in passing, are words never used in Scotland; they are exotic English terms. The mantle of the hero in verse third recalls that of Gil Morrice, which was 'a' gowd but the hem'—a specialty, we may say, not likely to have occurred to a male mind. What the wily lord does in verse fifth is the exact counterpart of the account of the eldern knight in *Sir Patrick Spence*:

Up and spak an eldern knight,
Sat at the king's right knee.

Observe the description of the king's jealous rage in *Young Waters*; how perfectly the same is that of the baron in *Gil Morrice*:

Then up and spak the bauld baron,
An angry man was he * *
'Nae wonder, nae wonder, Gil Morrice,
My lady lo'es thee weel,
The fairest part of my bodie
Is blacker than thy heel.'

Even in so small a matter as the choice of rhymes, especially where there is any irregularity, it may be allowable to point out a parallelism. Is there not such between those in the verse descriptive of Young Waters's fettering, and those in the closing stanza of *Sir Patrick Spence*? It belongs to the idiosyncrasy of an author to make *feet* rhyme twice over to *deep*. Finally, let us observe how like the tone as well as words of the last lines of *Young Waters* to a certain verse in *Hardyknute*:

The fainting corps of warriors lay,
Ne'er to rise again.

Percy surmised that *Young Waters* related to the fate of the Earl of Moray, slain by the Earl of Huntly in 1592, not without the concurrence, as was suspected, of the king, whose jealousy, it has been surmised, was excited against the young noble by indiscreet expressions of the queen. To the same subject obviously referred the ballad of the *Bonny Earl of Murray*, which consists, however, of but six stanzas, the last of which is very like the second of *Young Waters*:

O lang will his lady
Look ower the Castle Downe,
Ere she see the Earl of Murray
Come sounding through the town.

Edom o' Gordon is only a modern and improved version of an old ballad which Percy found in his folio manuscript under the name of *Captain Adam Carre*. It clearly relates to a frightful act of Adam Gordon of Auchindown, when he maintained Queen Mary's interest in the north in 1571—the burning of the house of Towie, with the lady and her family within it. All that can be surmised here is that the revision was the work of the same pen with the pieces here cited—as witness, for example, the opening stanzas:

It fell about the Martinmas,
When the wind blew shrill and cauld, [14]
Said Edom o' Gordon to his men:
'We maun draw till a hauld.
'And what a hauld shall we draw till,
My merry men and me?
We will gae to the house o' Rodes,
To see that fair ladye.'
The lady stood on her castle-wa',
Beheld baith dale and down;
There she was 'ware of a host of men
Come riding towards the town. [15]
'O see ye not, my merry men a', [16]
O see ye not what I see?' &c.

In the *Jew's Daughter* there is much in the general style to remind us of others of this group of ballads; but there are scarcely any parallel expressions. One may be cited:

She rowed him in a cake of lead,
Bade him lie still and sleep,
She cast him in a deep draw-well,
Was fifty fadom deep.

This must remind the reader of *Sir Patrick Spence*:

Half ower, half ower to Aberdour,
It's fifty fathom deep.

---

[14] *Young Waters* opens in the same manner:
About Yule, when the wind blew cool.

[15] We have seen the same description in both *Young Waters* and the *Bonny Earl of Murray*.

[16] Compare this with *Sir Patrick Spence*:
'Mak haste, mak haste, my merry men a'.'

Gilderoy, in the version printed by Percy, is a ballad somewhat peculiar, in a rich dulcet style, and of very smooth versification, but is only an improved version of a rude popular ballad in the same measure, which was printed in several collections long before, [17]_and was probably a street-ditty called forth by the hanging of the real robber, Patrick Macgregor, commonly called Gilderoy, [18]in 1636. The concluding verses of the refined version recall the peculiar manner of the rest of these poems:

Gif Gilderoy had done amiss,
He might hae banished been;
Ah what sair cruelty is this,
To hang sic handsome men:
To hang the flower o' Scottish land,
Sae sweet and fair a boy;
Nae lady had sae white a hand
As thee, my Gilderoy.
Of Gilderoy sae 'fraid they were,
They bound him mickle strong;
Till Edinburgh they led him there,
And on a gallows hung:
They hung him high aboon the rest,
He was sae trim a boy;
There died the youth whom I lo'ed best,
My handsome Gilderoy.
Thus having yielded up his breath,
I bare his corpse away;,
With tears that trickled for his death,
I washed his comely clay.,
And sicker in a grave sae deep,
I laid the dear-lo'ed boy;,
And now for ever maun I weep
My winsome Gilderoy.

---

[17] In a *Collection of Old Ballads,* printed for J. Roberts, London, 1723; also in Thomson's *Orpheus Caledonius,* 1733.
[18] The appellative, Gilderoy, means the ruddy-complexioned lad.

If any one will compare the Percy version of this ballad with the homely and indecorous ones printed before, he will not be the more disposed to go back to antiquity and a humble grade of authorship for what is best in the Scottish ballads.[19]

Edward, Edward, which Percy received from Sir David Dalrymple, and placed among his oldest pieces, in affectedly old spelling, is a striking melodramatic composition:

'Why does your brand sae drap wi' bluid,
Edward, Edward?,
Why does your brand sae drap wi' bluid,
And why sae sad gang ye, O?',
'O, I hae killed my hawk sae guid,,
Mother, mother:,
O, I hae killed my hawk sae guid,,
And I had nae mair but he, O.'
'Your hawk's bluid was never sae reid,,
Edward, Edward;,
Your hawk's bluid was never sae reid,,
My dear son, I tell ye, O.',
'O, I hae killed my reid-roan steed,,
Mother, mother;,
O, I hae killed my reid-roan steed,,
That erst was sae fair and free, O.'
'Your steed was auld, and ye hae gat mair,,
Edward, Edward;,

---

[19] Professor Aytoun says of this ballad, that 'it was adapted from the original by Sir Alexander Halket—at least, such was the general understanding until lately, when it became a mania with some literary antiquaries [a glance at the opinions of the present writer] to attribute the authorship of the great bulk of the Scottish ballads to Sir Alexander's sister, Lady Wardlaw, on the single ground that she was the composer of *Hardyknute*.' My learned friend is here very unlucky, for Lady Wardlaw had no brother, nor does any Sir Alexander Halket appear in her family history. This, however, is not all. It was a song to the *tune of Gilderoy* which was attributed to Sir Alexander Halket (Johnson's *Scots Musical Museum*)—namely, the well-known *Ah, Chloris,* which turns out to be a composition of Sir Charles Sedley, inserted by him in a play entitled the *Mulberry Garden,* which was acted in 1668.

Your steed was auld, and ye hae gat mair,,
Some other dool ye drie, O.',
'O, I hae killed my father dear,,
Mother, mother;,
O, I hae killed my father dear,,
Alas, and wae is me, O.'
'And whaten penance will ye drie for that,,
Edward, Edward?,
And whaten penance will ye drie for that,,
My dear son, now tell me, O?',
'I'll set my feet in yonder boat,,
Mother, mother;,
I'll set my feet in yonder boat,,
And I'll fare over the sea, O.'

* * *

'And what will ye leave to your bairns and your wife,,
Edward, Edward?,
And what will ye leave to your bairns and your wife,,
When ye gang over the sea, O?',
'The warld's room, let them beg through life,,
Mother, mother;,
The warld's room, let them beg through life,,
For them never mair will I see, O.'
'And what will ye leave to your ain mother dear,,
Edward, Edward;,
And what will ye leave to your ain mother dear,,
My dear son, now tell me, O?',
'The curse of hell frae me sall ye bear,,
Mother, mother;,
The curse of hell frae me sall ye bear,,
Sic counsels ye gave me, O.'

It seems unaccountable how any editor of Percy's discernment could ever have accepted this as old poetry. There is certainly none prior to 1700 which exhibits this kind of diction. Neither did any such poetry at any time proceed from a rustic uneducated mind.

When we continue our search beyond the bounds of Percy's *Reliques*, we readily find ballads passing as old, which are not unlike the above, either in regard to their general beauty, or special strains of thought and expression. There are five which seem peculiarly liable to suspicion on both grounds—namely, *Johnie of Bradislee, Mary Hamilton,* the *Gay Gos-hawk, Fause Foodrage,* and the *Lass o' Lochryan.*

In *Johnie o' Bradislee,* the hero is a young unlicensed huntsman, who goes out to the deer-forest against his mother's advice, and has a fatal encounter with seven foresters. Observe the description of the youth:

His cheeks were like the roses red,
His neck was like the snaw;
He was the bonniest gentleman
My eyes they ever saw.
His coat was o' the scarlet red,
His vest was o' the same;
His stockings were o' the worset lace,
And buckles tied to the same.
The shirt that was upon his back
Was o' the Holland fine;
The doublet that was over that
Was o' the Lincoln twine.
The buttons that were upon his sleeve
Were o' the gowd sae guid, &c.

This is mercery of the eighteenth, and no earlier century. Both Gilderoy and Gil Morrice are decked out in a similar fashion; and we may fairly surmise that it was no man's mind which revelled so luxuriously in the description of these three specimens of masculine beauty, or which invested them in such elegant attire. Johnie kills the seven foresters, but receives a deadly hurt. He then speaks in the following strain:

'O is there a bird in a' this bush
Would sing as I would say,
Go home and tell my auld mother
That I hae won the day?

'Is there ever a bird in a' this bush
Would sing as I would say,
Go home and tell my ain true love
To come and fetch Johnie away?
'Is there a bird in this hale forest
Would do as mickle for me,
As dip its wing in the wan water,
And straik it ower my ee-bree?'
The starling flew to his mother's bower-stane,
It whistled and it sang;
And aye the owerword o' its tune
Was, 'Johnie tarries lang.'
The mother says in conclusion:
'Aft hae I brought to Bradislee
The less gear and the mair;
But I ne'er brought to Bradislee
What grieved my heart sae sair.'

Now, first, is not the literary beauty of the above expressions of the young huntsman calculated to excite suspicion? It may be asked, is there anything in the older Scottish poets comparable to them? Second, how like is the verse regarding the starling to one in *Gil Morrice*!

Gil Morrice sat in guid green wood,
He whistled and he sang;
'O what mean a' the folk coming?
My mother tarries lang.'

Then, as to the last verse, how like to one in *Young Waters*!

Aft hae I ridden through Stirling town,
In the wind both and the rain,
But I ne'er rade through Stirling town
Ne'er to return again.

Mary Hamilton describes the tragic fate of an attendant on Queen Mary, brought to the gallows for destroying her own infant. The reflections of the heroine at the last sad moment are expressed in the same rich strain of sentiment as some of the passages of other ballads already quoted, and with remarkable parallelisms in terms:

'O aften hae I dressed my queen,
And put gowd in her hair;
But now I've gotten for my reward
The gallows tree to share.

* * *

'I charge ye all, ye mariners,
When ye sail ower the faem,
Let neither my father nor mother get wit
But that I 'm coming hame.

* * *

'O little did my mother think
That day she cradled me,
What lands I was to travel ower,
What death I was to die!'

The Scottish ladies sit bewailing the loss of Sir Patrick Spence's companions, 'wi' the gowd kaims in their hair.' Sir Patrick tells his friends before starting on his voyage, 'Our ship must sail the faem;' and in the description of the consequences of his shipwreck, we find 'Mony was the feather-bed that flattered on the faem.' No old poet would use foam as an equivalent for the sea; but it was just such a phrase as a poet of the era of Pope would love to use in that sense. The first of the above verses is evidently a cast from the same mould of thought as Bradislee's mother's concluding lament, and Young Waters's last words just quoted. The resemblance is not of that kind which arises from the use of literary commonplaces or stock phrases: the expressions have that identity which betrays their common source in one mind, a mind having a great command of rich and simple pathos.

In the *Gay Gos-hawk*, a gentleman commissions the bird to go on a mission to his mistress, who is secluded from him among her relations, and tell her how he dies by long waiting for her; whereupon she returns an answer by the same messenger, to the effect that she will presently meet him at Mary's Kirk for the effecting of their nuptials. The opening of the poem is just a variation of Bradislee's apostrophe to *his* bird-messenger:

'O waly, waly, my gay gos-hawk,
Gin your feathering be sheen!'
'And waly, waly, my master dear,
Gin ye look pale and lean!
'Oh, have ye tint at tournament
Your sword, or yet your spear?
Or mourn ye for the southern lass,
Whom ye may not win near?'
'I have not tint at tournament
My sword, nor yet my spear;
But sair I mourn for my true love,
Wi' mony a bitter tear.
'But weel's me on you, my gay gos-hawk,
Ye can both speak and flie;
Ye sall carry a letter to my love,
Bring an answer back to me.'

Hardyknute, *Sir Patrick Spence*, and *Gil Morrice*, all open, it will be recollected, with the sending away of a message. Here is a fourth instance, very like one artist's work, truly.

The lover describes his mistress in terms recalling *Bradislee*:

'The red that is on my true love's cheek
Is like blood-draps on the snaw;
The white that is on her breast bare,
Like the down o' the white sea-maw.'

The bird arrives at the lady's abode:

And first he sang a low, low note,
And syne he sang a clear;
And aye the owerword o' the sang
Was, 'Your love can no win here.'

Gil Morrice has:

Aye the owerword o' his sang
Was, 'My mother tarries lang.'

The lady feigns death, after the device of Juliet:

Then up and rose her seven brethren,

And hewed to her a bier;
They hewed frae the solid aik,
Laid it ower wi' silver clear.
Then up and gat her seven sisters,
And sewed to her a kell;
And every steek that they put in
Sewed to a silver bell.

Here we have the same style of luxurious description of which we have already seen so many examples—so different from the usually bald style of the real homely ballads of the people. It is, further, very remarkable that in *Clerk Saunders* it is seven brothers of the heroine who come in and detect her lover; and in the *Douglas Tragedy*, when the pair are eloping, Lord William spies his mistress's

... seven brethren bold
Come riding o'er the lee.

Both of these ballads, indeed, shew a structure and a strain of description and sentiment justifying the strongest suspicions of their alleged antiquity, and pointing to the same source as the other pieces already noticed.

The ballad of *Fause Foodrage*, which Sir Walter Scott printed for the first time, describes a successful conspiracy by Foodrage and others against King Honour and his queen. The king being murdered, the queen is told, that if she brings forth a son, it will be put to death likewise; so she escapes, and, bringing a male child into the world, induces the lady of Wise William to take charge of it as her own, while she herself takes charge of the lady's daughter. The unfortunate queen then arranges a future conduct for both parties, in language violently figurative:

'And ye maun learn my gay gos-hawk,
Right weel to breast a steed;
And I sall learn your turtle-dow
As weel to write and read.
'And ye maun learn my gay gos-hawk,
To wield both bow and brand;
And I sall learn your turtle-dow

To lay gowd wi' her hand.
'At kirk and market, when we meet,
We'll dare make nae avowe,
But—Dame, how does my gay gos-hawk?
Madam, how does my dow?'

When the royal youth grows up, Wise William reveals to him his history, and how his mother is still in confinement in Foodrage's hands. 'The boy stared wild like a gray gos-hawk' at hearing the strange intelligence, but soon resolves on a course of action:

He has set his bent bow to his breast,
And leapt the castle-wa',
And soon he has seized on Fause Foodrage,
Wha loud for help 'gan ca'.

The slaying of Foodrage and marriage of the turtle-dow wind up the ballad. Now, is not the adoption of the term, 'gay gos-hawk' in this ballad, calculated to excite a very strong suspicion as to a community of authorship with the other, in which a gay gos-hawk figures so prominently? But this is not all. 'The boy stared wild like a gray gos-hawk,' is nearly identical with a line of *Hardyknute*:

Norse e'en like gray gos-hawk stared wild.

Scott was roused by this parallelism into suspicion of the authenticity of the ballad, and only tranquillised by finding a lady of rank who remembered hearing in her infancy the verses which have here been quoted. He felt compelled, he tells us, 'to believe that the author of *Hardyknute* copied from the old ballad, if the coincidence be not altogether accidental.' Finally, the young prince's procedure in storming the castle, is precisely that of Gil Morrice in gaining access to that of Lord Barnard:

And when he cam to Barnard's yett,
He would neither chap nor ca',
But set his bent bow to his breast,
And lightly lap the wa'.

It may fairly be said that, in ordinary literature, coincidences like this are never 'accidental.' It may be observed, much of the narration in *Fause Foodrage* is in a stiff and somewhat hard style, recalling *Hardyknute.* It was probably one of the earlier compositions of its author.

The *Lass o' Lochryan* describes the hapless voyage of a maiden mother in search of her love Gregory. In the particulars of sea-faring and the description of the vessel, *Sir Patrick Spence* is strongly recalled.

She has garred build a bonny ship;
It's a' covered o'er wi' pearl;
And at every needle-tack was in't
There hung a siller bell.

Let the reader revert to the description of the bier prepared for the seeming dead lady in the *Gay Gos-hawk.*

She had na sailed a league but twa,
Or scantly had she three,
Till she met wi' a rude rover,
Was sailing on the sea.

The reader will remark in *Sir Patrick*:

They had na sailed a league, a league,
A league but barely three, &c.

The rover asks:

'Now, whether are ye the queen hersel,
Or ane o' her Maries three,
Or are ye the Lass o' Lochryan,
Seeking love Gregory?' [20]

The queen's Maries are also introduced in *Mary Hamilton,* who, indeed, is represented as one of them:

Yestreen the queen she had four Maries;
The night, she has but three;
There was Mary Seton and Mary Beaton,
And Mary Carmichael and me.

On arriving at love Gregory's castle, beside the sea, the lady calls:

'Oh, open the door, love Gregory;

---

[20] The above three verses are in the version printed in Lawrie and Symington's collection, 1791.

Oh, open and let me in;
For the wind blaws through my yellow hair,
And the rain draps o'er my chin.'

He being in a dead sleep, his mother answers for him, and turns from the door the forlorn applicant, who then exclaims:

'Tak down, tak down the mast o' gowd;
Set up a mast o' tree;
It disna become a forsaken lady
To sail sae royallie.

'Tak down, tak down the sails o' silk;
Set up the sails o' skin;
Ill sets the outside to be gay,
When there's sic grief within.'

Gregory then awakes:

O quickly, quickly raise he up,
And fast ran to the strand,
And there he saw her, fair Annie,
Was sailing frae the land.

* * *

The wind blew loud, the sea grew rough,
And dashed the boat on shore;
Fair Annie floated on the faem,
But the babie raise no more.

* * *

And first he kissed her cherry cheek,
And syne he kissed her chin;
And syne he kissed her rosy lips—
There was nae breath within.

The resemblance of these verses to several of the preceding ballads,[21] and particularly to *Sir Patrick Spence*, and their superiority in delicacy of feeling and in diction to all ordinary ballad poetry, is very striking. It chances that there is here, as in

---

[21] A passage in *Hardyknute* maybe quoted as bearing a marked resemblance to one of the above verses:

Take aff, take aff his costly jupe,
Of gold well was it twined, &c.

Sir Patrick, one word peculiarly *detective*—namely, strand, as meaning the shore. In the Scottish language, strand means a rivulet, or a street-gutter—never the margin of the sea.

There is a considerable number of other ballads which are scarcely less liable to suspicion as modern compositions, and which are all marked more or less by the peculiarities seen in the above group. Several of them are based, like the one just noticed, on irregular love, which they commonly treat with little reproach, and usually with a romantic tenderness. *Willie and May Margaret*[22]describes a young lover crossing the Clyde in a flood to see his mistress, and as denied access by her mother in a feigned voice, after which he is drowned in recrossing the river; the ballad being thus a kind of counterpart of the *Lass of Lochryan.* In *Young Huntin,* otherwise called *Earl Richard,* the hero is killed in his mistress's bower through jealousy, and we have then a verse of wonderful power—such as no rustic and unlettered bard ever wrote, or ever will write:

'O slowly, slowly wanes the night,
And slowly daws the day:
There is a dead man in my bower,
I wish he were away.'

One called *Fair Annie* relates how a mistress won upon her lover, and finally gained him as a husband, by patience, under the trial of seeing a new bride brought home. [23]In the latter, the behaviour of the patient mistress is thus described:

O she has served the lang tables
Wi' the white bread and the wine;
And aye she drank the wan water,
To keep her colour fine.

---

[22] Called, in Professor Aytoun's collection, *The Mother's Malison*; and in Mr Buchan's, *The Drowned Lovers.*

[23] A ballad named *Burd Ellen,* resembling *Fair Annie* in the general cast of the story, is a Scottish modification of the ballad of *Child Waters,* published by Percy, from his folio manuscript, 'with some corrections.' It probably came through the same mill as *Gil Morrice,* though with less change—a conjecture rendered the more probable, for reasons to be seen afterwards, from its having been obtained by Mr Jamieson from Mrs Brown of Falkland.

The expression, the wan water, occurs in several of this group of ballads. Thus, in *Johnie of Bradislee*:

Is there ever a bird in this hale forest
Will do as mickle for me,
As dip its wing in the wan water,
And straik it o'er my ee-bree?

And in the *Douglas Tragedy*:

O they rade on, and on they rade,
And a' by the light o' the moon,
Until they cam to yon wan water,
And there they lighted down.

See further in *Young Huntin*:

And they hae ridden along, along,
All the long summer's tide,
Until they came to the wan water,
The deepest place in Clyde.

The circumstance is very suspicious, for we find this phrase in no other ballads.

In *Clerk Saunders*, the hero is slain in his mistress's bower, by the rage of one of her seven brothers, whose act is described in precisely the same terms as the slaughter of *Gil Morrice* by the bold baron:

He's ta'en out his trusty brand,
And straikt it on the strae,
And through and through Clerk Saunders' side
He's gart it come and gae. [24]

Sweet William's Ghost, a fine superstitious ballad, first published in Ramsay's *Tea-table Miscellany*, 1724, is important as the earliest printed of all the Scottish ballads after the admittedly modern *Hardyknute*:

There came a ghost to Margaret's door,
With many a grievous groan;

---

[24] Now he has ta'en his trusty brand,
And slait it on the strae,
And through Gil Morrice's fair bodie
He garred cauld iron gae.—*Gil Morrice*.

And aye he tirled at the pin,
But answer made she none.

* * *

'O sweet Margaret! O dear Margaret!
I pray thee, speak to me;
Give me my faith and troth, Margaret,
As I gave it to thee.'
'Thy faith and troth thou 's never get,
Nor yet will I thee lend,
Till that thou come within my bower,
And kiss my cheek and chin.' [25]
'If I should come within thy bower,
I am no earthly man;
And should I kiss thy rosy lips,
Thy days will not be lang.

* * *

'My bones are buried in yon kirk-yard,
Afar beyond the sea;
And it is but my spirit, Margaret,
That's now speaking to thee.'
She stretched out her lily hand,
And for to do her best,
'Ha'e there's your faith and troth, Willie;
God send your soul good rest.'
Now she has kilted her robes of green
A piece below her knee,
And a' the live-lang winter night,
The dead corp followed she.
'Is there any room at your head, Willie,
Or any room at your feet?

---

[25] And first he kissed her cherry cheek,
And syne he kissed her chin;
And syne he kissed her rosy lips—
There was nae breath within.—*Lass o' Lochryan.*
To kiss cheek and chin in succession is very peculiar; and it is by such peculiar ideas that identity of authorship is indicated.

Or any room at your side, Willie,
Wherein that I may creep?'
'There's no room at my head, Margaret;
There's no room at my feet;
There's no room at my side, Margaret;
My coffin's made so meet.' [26]
Then up and crew the red, red cock,
And up then crew the gray,
''Tis time, 'tis time, my dear Margaret,
That you were going away.'

* * *

So far, the ballad appears as composed in the style of those already noticed—a style at once simple and poetical—neither shewing the rudeness of the common peasant's ballad, nor the formal refinement of the modern English poet. But next follow two stanzas, which manifestly have been patched on by some contemporary of Ramsay:

No more the ghost to Margaret said,
But with a grievous groan
Evanished in a cloud of mist,
And left her all alone, &c.

No such conclusion, perhaps, was needed, for it may be suspected that the verse here printed *sixth* is the true *finale* of the story, accidentally transferred from its proper place.

There is a slight affinity between the above and a ballad entitled *Tam Lane*, to which Scott drew special attention in his *Border Minstrelsy*, by making it a peg for eighty pages of prose dissertation *On the Fairies of Popular Superstition*. It describes a lover as lost to his mistress, by being reft away into fairy-land, and as recovered by an effort of courage and presence of mind on her part. It opens thus:

O I forbid ye maidens a',
That wear gowd in your hair,
To come or gae by Carterhaugh,
For the young Tam Lane is there.

---

[26] That is, so exactly measured.

It may be remarked how often before we have seen maidens described as wearing gold in their hair. One maiden defies the prohibition:

Janet has kilted her green kirtle
A little aboon her knee,
And she has braided her yellow hair
A little aboon her bree.

This, it will be observed, is all but the very same description applied to Margaret in the preceding ballad. The narrative goes on:

She had na pu'd a red, red rose,
A rose but barely three,
Till up and starts a wee, wee man
At Lady Janet's knee.

Remember Sir Patrick's voyage:

They had na sailed a league, a league,
A league but barely three.

Let it also here be noted that the eldern knight in that ballad sits 'at the king's knee,' and the nurse in *Gil Morrice* is not very necessarily described as having 'the bairn upon her knee.' Why the knee on these occasions, if not a habitual idea of one poet?[27]

The consequences of the visit having been fatal to Lady Janet's health and peace, she goes back to see her elfin lover, Tam Lane, who instructs her how to recover him from his bondage to the queen of fairy-land.

'The night it is good Halloween,
When fairy folk will ride;
And they that wad their true love win,
At Miles Cross they maun bide.'
'But how shall I thee ken, Tam Lane,

[27] In *Childe Maurice*, in Percy's folio manuscript, the hero says:
'... come hither, thou little foot-page,
That runneth lowly by my knee.'
The author of *Sir Patrick Spence*, and the other ballads in question, might have known this version, and from it caught this expression.

Or how shall I thee knaw,
Amang so many unearthly knights,
The like I never saw?'
'The first company that passes by,
Say na, and let them gae;
The next company that passes by,
Say na, and do right sae;
The third company that passes by,
Then I'll be ane o' thae.
'First let pass the black, Janet,
And syne let pass the brown;
But grip ye to the milk-white steed,
And pu' the rider down.'

Compare the first two of these stanzas with the queries put by the gay gos-hawk to his master:

'But how shall I your true love find,
Or how suld I her know?
I bear a tongue ne'er wi' her spoke,
An eye that ne'er her saw.'
'O weel sall ye my true love ken,
Sae sore as ye her see,' &c.

As to the latter three stanzas, they exhibit a formula of description, which appears in several of the suspected ballads, consisting of a series of nearly identical statements, apparently for the sake of amplitude. For example, the progress of the seeming funeral of the lady in the *Gay Gos-hawk*:

At the first kirk of fair Scotland,
They gart the bells be rung;
At the second kirk of fair Scotland,
They gart the mass be sung.
At the third kirk of fair Scotland,
They dealt gold for her sake;
And the fourth kirk of fair Scotland,
Her true love met them at.

Or the following, in *Sweet Willie and Fair Annie*, which is almost the same incident and relation of circumstances as the said seeming funeral; only the lady in this case is dead:

The firsten bower that he cam till,
There was right dowie wark;
Her mother and her sisters three
Were making to Annie a sark.
The next bower that he cam till,
There was right dowie cheer;
Her father and her seven brethren
Were making to Annie a bier.
The lasten bower that he cam till,
O heavy was his care;
The waxen lights were burning bright,
And fair Annie streekit there.

In Scott's version of *Tam Lane* there are some stanzas of so modern a cast as to prove that this poem has been at least tampered with. For example, the account of fairy life:

'And all our wants are well supplied
From every rich man's store,
Who thankless sins the gifts he gets,
And vainly grasps for more.'

Without regard, however, to such manifest patches, the general structure and style of expression must be admitted to strongly recall the other ballads which have been already commented on.

Only a wish to keep this dissertation within moderate bounds forbids me to analyse a few other ballads, as the *Douglas Tragedy, Sweet Willie and Fair Annie, Lady Maiery,* the *Clerk's Two Sons of Owsenford,* and a Scotch *Heir of Linne* lately recovered by Mr J. H. Dixon, all of which, besides others which must rest unnamed, bear traces of the same authorship with the ballads already brought under notice.

It is now to be remarked of the ballads published by the successors of Percy, as of those which he published, that there is not a particle of positive evidence for their having existed before the eighteenth century. Overlooking the one given by Ramsay in his *Tea-table Miscellany*, we have neither print nor manuscript of them before the reign of George III. They are not in the style of old literature. They contain no references to old literature. As little does old literature contain any references to them. They wholly escaped the collecting diligence of Bannatyne. James Watson, who published a collection of Scottish poetry in 1706-1711, wholly overlooks them. Ramsay, as we see, caught up only one. Even Herd, in 1769, only gathered a few fragments of some of these poems. It was reserved for Sir Walter Scott and Robert Jamieson, at the beginning of the nineteenth century, to obtain copies of the great bulk of these poems—that is, the ballads over and above the few published by Percy—from a lady—a certain 'Mrs Brown of Falkland,' who seems to have been the wife of the Rev. Andrew Brown, minister of that parish in Fife—is known to have been the daughter of Professor Thomas Gordon, of King's College, Aberdeen—and is stated to have derived her stores of legendary lore from the memory of her aunt, a Mrs Farquhar, the wife of a small proprietor in Braemar, who had spent the best part of her life among flocks and herds, but lived latterly in Aberdeen. At the suggestion of Mr William Tytler, a son of Mrs Brown wrote down a parcel of the ballads which her aunt had heard in her youth from the recitation of nurses and old women. [28]Such were the external circumstances, none of them giving the least support to the assumed antiquity of the pieces, but rather exciting some suspicion to the contrary effect.

When we come to consider the internal evidence, what do we find? We find that these poems, in common with those published by Percy, are composed in a style of romantic beauty and elevation distinguishing them from all other remains of Scottish traditionary poetry. They are quite unlike the palpably old historical ballads, such as the *Battle of Otterbourne* and the *Raid of the Reidswire*. They are unlike the Border ballads, such as *Dick o' the Cow*, and *Jock o' the Syde*, commemorating domestic events of the latter part of the sixteenth century. They are

[28] *Minstrelsy Scot. Border*, I. cxxvi.

strikingly unlike the *Burning of Frendraught*, the *Bonny House o' Airly*, and the *Battle of Bothwell Bridge*, contemporaneous metrical chronicles of events of the seventeenth century. Not less different are they from a large mass of ballads, which have latterly been published by Mr Peter Buchan and others, involving romantic incidents, it is true, or eccentricities in private life, but in such rude and homely strains as speak strongly of a plebeian origin. In the ballads here brought under question, the characters are usually persons of condition, generally richly dressed, often well mounted, and of a dignified bearing towards all inferior people. The page, the nurse, the waiting-woman, the hound, the hawk, and other animals connected with the pageantry of high life, are prominently introduced. Yet the characters and incidents are alike relieved from all clear connection with any particular age: they may be said to form a world of their own, of no particular era, wherein the imagination of the reader may revel, as that of the author has done. It may be allowably said, there is a tone of *breeding* throughout these ballads, such as is never found in the productions of rustic genius. One marked feature—the pathos of deep female affections—the sacrifice and the suffering which these so often involve—runs through nearly the whole. References to religion and religious ceremonies and fanes are of the slightest kind. We hear of bells being rung and mass sung, but only to indicate a time of day. Had they been old ballads continually changing in diction and in thought, as passed down from one reciter to another, they could not have failed to involve some considerable trace of the intensely earnest religious life of the seventeenth century; but not the slightest tincture of this enthusiastic feeling appears in them, a defect the more marked, as they contain abundant allusion to the superstitions which survived into the succeeding time of religious indifference, and indeed some of their best *effects* rest in a dexterous treatment of these weird ideas. There is but one exception to what has been observed on the obscurity of the epoch pointed to for the incidents—the dresses, properties, and decorations, are sometimes of a modern cast. The writer—if we may be allowed to speculate on a single writer—seems to have been unable to resist an inclination to indulge in description of the external furnishings of the heroes and heroines, or rather, perhaps, has been desirous of making out *effect* from these particulars; but the finery of the court of Charles II. is the furthest point reached in the retrospect—although, I must admit, this is in general treated with a vagueness that helps much to conceal the want of learning.

Another point of great importance in the matter of internal evidence, is the isolatedness of these ballads in respect of English traditionary literature. The Scottish muse has not always gone hand in hand with the English in point of time, but she has done so in all other respects. Any literature we had from the beginning of the seventeenth century downwards, was always sensibly tinged by what had immediately before been in vogue in the south. Nor is it easy to see how a people occupying part of the same island, and speaking essentially the same language, should have avoided this communion of literary taste; but the ballads in question are wholly unlike any English ballads. Look over Percy, Evans, or Mr Collier's suite of *Roxburghe Ballads*, giving those which were popular in London during the seventeenth century, and you find not a trace of the style and manner of these Scottish romantic ballads. Neither, it would appear, had one of them found its way into popularity in England before the time of Percy; for, had it been otherwise, he would have found them either in print or in the mouths of the people. [29]

Upon all of these considerations, I have arrived at the conclusion, that the high-class romantic ballads of Scotland are not ancient compositions—are not older than the early part of

---

[29] Robert Jamieson found in the *Kœmpe Viser*, a Danish collection of ballads published in 1695, one resembling the Scottish ballad of *Fair Annie* (otherwise called *Lady Jane*), and on this ground he became convinced that many of our traditionary ballads were of prodigious antiquity, though they had been intermediately subjected to many alterations. Mr Jamieson's belief seems remarkably ill supported, and as it has never obtained any adherents among Scottish ballad editors, I feel entitled to pass it over with but this slight notice.

the eighteenth century—and are mainly, if not wholly, the production of one mind.

Whose was this mind, is a different question, on which no such confident decision may for the present be arrived at; but I have no hesitation in saying that, from the internal resemblances traced on from *Hardyknute* through *Sir Patrick Spence* and *Gil Morrice* to the others, there seems to me a great *likelihood* that the whole were the composition of the authoress of that poem—namely, Elizabeth Lady Wardlaw of Pitreavie.

It may be demanded that something should be done to verify, or at least support, the allegation here made as to the peculiar literary character of the suspected ballads. This is, of course, a point to be best made out by a perusal of the entire body of this class of compositions, and scarcely by any other means. Still, it is a difference so striking, that even to present one typical ballad of true rustic origin, could not fail to make a considerable impression on the reader, after he has read specimens of those which are here attributed to a higher source. Be it observed, when an uneducated person speaks of knights, lords, and kings, or of dames and damosels, he reduces all to one homely level. He indulges in no diplomatic periphrases. It is simply, the king said this, and the lord said that—this thing was done, and that thing was done—the catastrophe or *dénouement* comes by a single stroke. This we find in the true stall-ballads. A vulgar, prosaic, and drawling character pervades the whole class, with few exceptions—a fact which ought to give no surprise, for does not all experience shew, that literature of any kind, to have effect, requires for its production a mind of some cultivation, and really good verse flowing from an uninstructed source is what never was, is not now, and never will be? With these remarks, I usher in a typical ballad of the common class—one taken down many years ago from the singing of an old man in the south of Scotland:

JAMES HATELIE.

It fell upon a certain day,
When the king from home he chanced to be,

The king's jewels they were stolen all,
And they laid the blame on James Hatelie.
And he is into prison cast,
And I wat he is condemned to *dee*;
For there was not a man in all the court
To speak a word for James Hatelie.
But the king's eldest daughter she loved him well,
But known her love it might not be;
And she has stolen the prison keys,
And gane in and discoursed wi' James Hatelie.
'Oh, did you steal them, James?' she said;
'Oh, did not you steal them, come tell to me?
For I'll make a vow, and I'll keep it true,
You's never be the worse of me.'
'I did not steal them,' James he said;
'And neither was it intended by me,
For the English they stole them themselves,
And I wat they've laid the blame on me.'
Now she has hame to her father gane,
And bowed her low down on her knee,
'I ask—I ask—I ask, father,' she said,
'I ask—I ask a boon of thee;
I never asked one in my life,
And one of them you must grant to me.'
'Ask on, ask on, daughter,' he said;
'And aye weel answered ye shall be;
For if it were my whole estate,
Naysaid, naysaid you shall not be.'
'I ask none of your gold, father,
As little of your white monie;
But all the asken that I do ask,
It is the life of James Hatelie.'
'Ask on, ask on, daughter,' he said;
'And aye weel answered ye shall be;
For I'll mak a vow, and keep it true—
James Hatelie shall not hanged be.'

'Another asken I ask, father;
Another asken I ask of thee—
Let Fenwick and Hatelie go to the sword,
And let them try their veritie.'
'Ask on, ask on, daughter,' he said;
'And aye weel answered you shall be;
For before the morn at twelve o'clock,
They both at the point of the sword shall be.'
James Hatelie was eighteen years of age,
False Fenwick was thirty years and three;
He lap about, and he strack about,
And he gave false Fenwick wounds three.
'Oh, hold your hand, James Hatelie,' he said;
'And let my breath go out and in;
Were it not for the spilling of my noble blood
And the shaming of my noble kin.
'Oh, hold your hand, James Hatelie,' he said;
Oh, hold your hand, and let me be;
For I'm the man that stole the jewels,
And a shame and disgrace it was to me.'
Then up bespoke an English lord,
I wat but he spoke haughtilie:
'I would rather have lost all my lands,
Before they had not hanged James Hatelie.'
Then up bespoke a good Scotch lord,
I wat a good Scotch lord was he:
'I would rather have foughten to the knees in blood,
Than they had hanged James Hatelie.'
Then up bespoke the king's eldest son:
'Come in, James Hatelie, and dine with me;
For I'll make a vow, and I'll keep it true—
You'se be my captain by land and sea.'
Then up bespoke the king's eldest daughter:
'Come in, James Hatelie, and dine with me;
For I'll make a vow, and I'll keep it true—
I'll never marrie a man but thee.'

Here is love, and here is innocence in difficulties—two things of high moral interest; yet how homely is the whole narration; how unlike the strains of the ballads which have been passed before the reader's view! And be it observed, the theory as to our ballads is, that they have been transmitted from old time, undergoing modifications from the minds of nurses, and other humble reciters, as they came along. If so, they ought to have presented the same plebeian strain of ideas and phraseology as *James Hatelie*; but we see they do not: they are, on the contrary, remarkably poetical, pure, and dignified.

Here I may, once for all, in opposition to Professor Aytoun and others, express my belief that the ballads in question are for the most part printed nearly, and, in some instances, entirely, in the condition in which they were left by the author. In *Edward*, I question if a line has been corrupted or a word altered. *Sir Patrick Spence* and *Gilderoy* are both so rounded and complete, so free, moreover, from all vulgar terms, that I feel nearly equally confident about them. All those which Percy obtained in manuscripts from Scotland, are neat finished compositions, as much so as any ballad of Tickell or Shenstone. Those from Mrs Brown's manuscript have also an author's finish clearly impressed on them. It is a mere assumption that they have been sent down, with large modifications, from old times. Had it been true, the ballads would have been full of vulgarisms, as we find to be the condition of certain of them which Peter Buchan picked up among the common people, after (shall we say) seventy or eighty years of traditionary handling. Now, no such depravation appears in the versions printed by Percy, Scott, and Jamieson.

It may be objected to the arguments founded on the great number of parallel passages, that these are but the stock phraseology of all ballad-mongers, and form no just proof of unity of authorship. If this were true, it might be an objection of some force; but it is not true. The *formulæ* in question are to be found hardly at all in any of the rustic or homely ballads. They are not to be found in any ballads which there is good reason to believe so old as the early part of the seventeenth century. They are to be found in no ballads which may even doubtfully be affiliated to England. All this, of course, can only be fully ascertained by a careful perusal of some large collection of ballads. Yet, even in such a case, a few examples may be viewed with interest, and not unprofitably. Of the plebeian ballads, a specimen has just been adduced. Let us proceed, then, to exemplify the ballads of the seventeenth century. First, take *Fair Margaret and Sweet William,* which Percy brought forward from a stall copy as, apparently, the ballad quoted in Fletcher's *Knight of the Burning Pestle*; though subjected to some alteration during the intermediate century and a half. It is as follows:

As it fell out on a long summer day,
Two lovers they sat on a hill;
They sat together that long summer day,
And could not take their fill.
'I see no harm by you, Margaret,
And you see none by me;
Before to-morrow at eight o'clock,
A rich wedding you shall see.'
Fair Margaret sat in her bouir window,
Combing her yellow hair;
There she spied sweit William and his bride,
As they were a-riding near.
Then doun she layed her ivorie combe,
And braided her hair in twain:
She went alive out of her bouir,
But never cam alive in't again.
When day was gone, and nicht was come,
And all men fast asleip,
Then came the spirit of fair Margaret,
And stood at William's feet.
'Are you awake, sweit William?' she said;
'Or, sweit William, are you asleip?
God give you joy of your gay bride-bed,
And me of my winding-sheet!'
When day was come, and nicht was gone,

And all men waked from sleip,
Sweit William to his lady said:
'My deir, I have cause to weep.
'I dreimt a dreim, my dear ladye;
Such dreims are never good:
I dreimt my bouir was full of red swine,
And my bride-bed full of blood.'
'Such dreims, such dreims, my honoured sir,
They never do prove good;
To dreim thy bouir was full of red swine,
And thy bride-bed full of blood.'
He called up his merry-men all,
By one, by two, and by three;
Saying: 'I'll away to fair Margaret's bouir,
By the leave of my ladye.'
And when he came to fair Margaret's bouir,
He knockit at the ring;
And who so ready as her seven brethren
To let sweit William in.
Then he turned up the covering sheet:
'Pray, let me see the deid;
Methinks, she looks all pale and wan;
She hath lost her cherry red.
'I'll do more for thee, Margaret,
Than any of thy kin,
For I will kiss thy pale wan lips,
Though a smile I cannot win.'
With that bespake the seven brethren,
Making most piteous moan:
'You may go kiss your jolly brown bride,
And let our sister alone.'
'If I do kiss my jolly brown bride,
I do but what is right;
I ne'er made a vow to yonder poor corpse,
By day nor yet by night.
'Deal on, deal on, my merry-men all;

Deal on your cake and your wine:
For whatever is dealt at her funeral to-day,
Shall be dealt to-morrow at mine.'
Fair Margaret died to-day, to-day,
Sweit William died to-morrow;
Fair Margaret died for pure true love,
Sweit William died for sorrow.
Margaret was buried in the lower chancel,
And William in the higher;
Out of her breast there sprang a rose,
And out of his a brier.
They grew till they grew unto the church-top,
And then they could grow no higher;
And there they tied in a true lovers' knot,
Which made all the people admire.
Then came the clerk of the parish,
As you the truth shall hear,
And by misfortune cut them down,
Or they had now been there.

Here, it will be observed, beyond the expression, 'my merry-men all,' there is no trace of the phraseology so marked in the group of ballads under our notice. Take, also, a ballad which, from the occurrences referred to, may be considered as antecedent to the epoch of *Hardyknute*, and we shall observe an equal, if not more complete, absence of the phraseology and manner of this class of ballads. It relates to a tragic love-story of 1631, as ascertained from the grave-stone of the heroine in the kirk-yard of Fyvie, Aberdeenshire:

Lord Fyvie had a trumpeter,
His name was Andrew Lammie;
He had the art to gain the heart
Of Mill-o'-Tifty's Annie.

* * *

She sighed sore, but said no more,
Alas, for bonny Annie!
She durst not own her heart was won

By the trumpeter of Fyvie.
At night when they went to their beds,
All slept full sound but Annie;
Love so opprest her tender breast,
Thinking on Andrew Lammie.
'Love comes in at my bed-side,
And love lies down beyond me,
Love has possessed my tender breast,
And wastes away my body.
'At Fyvie yetts there grows a flower,
It grows baith braid and bonny;
There is a daisy in the midst o' it.
And it's ca'd by Andrew Lammie.
'O gin that flower were in my breast,
For the love I bear the laddie,
I wad kiss it, and I wad clap it,
And daut it for Andrew Lammie.
'The first time I and my love met
Was in the woods of Fyvie;
His lovely form and speech so sweet
Soon gained the heart of Annie.
'Oh, up and down, in Tifty's den,
Where the burns run clear and bonny,
I've often gone to meet my love,
My bonny Andrew Lammie.
'He kissed my lips five thousand times,
And aye he ca'd me bonny;
And a' the answer he gat frae me,
Was, "My bonny Andrew Lammie!"'
But now, alas! her father heard
That the trumpeter of Fyvie
Had had the art to gain the heart
Of Tifty's bonny Annie.
And he has syne a letter wrote,
And sent it on to Fyvie,
To tell his daughter was bewitched

By his servant, Andrew Lammie.
When Lord Fyvie this letter read,
O dear, but he was sorry;
'The bonniest lass in Fyvie's land
Is bewitched by Andrew Lammie.'
Then up the stair his trumpeter
He called soon and shortly;
'Pray tell me soon what's this you've done
To Tifty's bonny Annie?'
'In wicked art I had no part,
Nor therein am I canny;
True love alone the heart has won
Of Tifty's bonny Annie.
'Woe betide Mill-o'-Tifty's pride,
For it has ruined many;
He'll no hae't said that she should wed
The trumpeter of Fyvie.'

* * *

'Love, I maun gang to Edinburgh;
Love, I maun gang and leave thee.'
She sighed sore, and said no more,
But, 'Oh, gin I were wi' ye!'
'I'll buy to thee a bridal goun;
My love, I'll buy it bonny!'
'But I'll be dead, ere ye come back
To see your bonny Annie.'
'If you'll be true, and constant too,
As my name's Andrew Lammie,
I shall thee wed when I come back,
Within the kirk of Fyvie.'
'I will be true, and constant too,
To thee, my Andrew Lammie;
But my bridal-bed will ere then be made
In the green kirk-yard of Fyvie.'
He hied him hame, and having spieled
To the house-top of Fyvie,

He blew his trumpet loud and shrill,
'Twas heard at Mill-o'-Tifty.
Her father locked the door at night,
Laid by the keys fu' canny;
And when he heard the trumpet sound,
Said: 'Your cow is lowing, Annie.'
'My father, dear, I pray forbear,
And reproach no more your Annie;
For I'd rather hear that cow to low
Than hae a' the kine in Fyvie.
'I would not for your braw new gown,
And a' your gifts sae many,
That it were told in Fyvie's land
How cruel you are to me.'
Her father struck her wondrous sore,
As also did her mother;
Her sisters always did her scorn,
As also did her brother.
Her brother struck her wondrous sore,
With cruel strokes and many;
He brak her back in the hall-door,
For loving Andrew Lammie.
'Alas, my father and mother dear,
Why are you so cruel to Annie?
My heart was broken first by love,
Now you have broken my bodie.
'Oh, mother dear, make ye my bed,
And lay my face to Fyvie;
There will I lie, and thus will die,
For my love, Andrew Lammie.'
Her mother she has made her bed,
And laid her face to Fyvie;
Her tender heart it soon did break,
And she ne'er saw Andrew Lammie.
When Andrew home from Edinburgh came,
With mickle grief and sorrow:

'My love has died for me to-day,
I'll die for her to-morrow.'
He has gone on to Tifty's den,
Where the burn runs clear and bonny;
With tears he viewed the Bridge of Heugh,
Where he parted last with Annie.
Then he has sped to the church-yard,
To the green church-yard of Fyvie;
With tears he watered his true love's grave,
And died for Tifty's Annie.

Let me repeat my acknowledgment that, while these extracts occupy more space than can well be spared, they form an imperfect means of establishing the negative evidence required in the case. But let the reader peruse the ballads of Buchan's collection known to relate to incidents of the seventeenth century, and he will find that they are all alike free from the favourite expressions of the unknown, or dimly known ballad-writer in question.

Let it never be objected that, if any one person living in the reigns of Queen Anne and George I. had composed so many fine poems, he or she could not have remained till now all but unknown. In the first half of the present century, there appeared in Scotland a series of fugitive pieces—songs—which attained a great popularity, without their being traced to any author. Every reader will remember *The Land of the Leal, Caller Herring, The Laird o' Cockpen, The Auld House*, and *He's ower the Hills that I lo'e weel.* It was not till after many years of fame that these pieces were found to be the production of a lady of rank, Carolina Baroness Nairn, who had passed through a life of seventy-nine years without being known as a song-writer to more than one person. It was the fate of this songstress to live in days when there was an interest felt in such authorships, insuring that she should sooner or later become known; but, had she lived a hundred years earlier, she might have died and left no sign, as I conjecture to have been the case with the author of this fine group of ballads; and future Burnses might have pondered over her productions, with endless regret that the names of their *authors* were 'buried among the wreck of things that were.'

If there be any truth or force in this speculation, I shall be permitted to indulge in the idea that a person lived a hundred years before Scott, who, with his feeling for Scottish history, and the features of the past generally, constructed out of these materials a similar romantic literature. In short, Scotland appears to have had a Scott a hundred years before the actual person so named. And we may well believe that if we had not had the first, we either should not have had the second, or he would have been something considerably different, for, beyond question, Sir Walter's genius was fed and nurtured on the ballad literature of his native country. From his *Old Mortality* and *Waverley*, back to his *Lady of the Lake and Marmion*; from these to his *Lay of the Last Minstrel*; from that to his *Eve of St John* and *Glenfinlas*; and from these, again, to the ballads which he collected, mainly the produce (as I surmise) of an individual precursor, is a series of steps easily traced, and which no one will dispute. Much significance there is, indeed, in his own statement, that *Hardyknute* was the first poem he ever learned, and the last he should forget. Its author—if my suspicion be correct—was his literary foster-mother, and we probably owe the direction of his genius, and all its fascinating results, primarily to her.

www.ingramcontent.com/pod-product-compliance
Lightning Source LLC
LaVergne TN
LVHW010545100826
845148LV00013B/2610

* 9 7 8 1 7 7 0 8 3 1 5 2 0 *